EARLY LEARNING EXPERIENCES IN SOCIAL STUDIES

by Imogene Forte and Joy MacKenzie

Incentive Publications, Inc.
Nashville, Tennessee

Illustrated by Gayle Seaberg Harvey
Cover Design by Marta Drayton
Edited by Leslie Britt

ISBN 0-86530-294-4

PRINTED IN THE UNITED STATES OF AMERICA

Table Of Contents

About This Book . . .

Early Learning Experiences in Social Studies has been planned to help young children learn through experimentation, through creative involvement in directed activities, and finally, through the joy of discovery.

Young children are curious about and extremely sensitive to their environment. They instinctively push and pull, take apart and attempt to put together again, smell, taste, feel, and listen to things around them. "Why?" "What?" "When?" "Where?" and "How?" are words they use naturally and often. It is this interaction with their environment that parents and teachers can either nurture and encourage or inhibit and retard. Children who have had many happy, satisfying opportunities to use their hands, feet, eyes, ears, and whole bodies are much more apt to adjust happily and successfully to more structured learning experiences.

The purpose of the activities in *Early Learning Experiences in Social Studies* is to help children acquire and make meaningful use of beginning social studies skills and to sort out and bring into focus scattered knowledge and isolated concepts.

The book includes a mix of hands-on experimentation, directed pencil-and-paper activities, and discussion activities. While instructions are directed to the child, an adult will, of course, need to read and interact with the child in the interpretation and completion of the activities. Ideally, the projects will be presented in a stress-free setting that will afford time for the child to question, explore, wonder, and ponder—and to develop an abiding, imaginatively inquisitive approach to social studies skills and concepts. Each activity is intended to contribute to the development of a sound foundation upon which the basic skills necessary for school readiness may be built. They have also been planned to provide a flexibility and freedom to enhance the child's growth in social studies and related areas, in environmental awareness, and in creative self-expression.

You are part of
a great big world,
made up of lots of
different kinds of people,
lots of different kinds of places,
and lots of different
kinds of things.

Which things can be found
in your part of the world?
Use a bright color
to circle the ones
you have seen.

My Name Is _____

Meet A Very Important Person!

You are a very important person in your world,
so introduce yourself!

Ask someone to help you make the large letters M E
from colored paper.
Tape them to a door or wall.
Write your name in large letters on the M.
Draw a picture of yourself on the E.
Fill the remaining space with pictures
that tell about yourself and that are important to you.

Make A Body Puzzle!

Lie down on a large sheet of paper. Ask someone to trace around your body.

Cut the picture apart to make a giant puzzle.

Now put yourself back together again!

All Through The Day

On this page you see many things you might do from the time you get up in the morning until you go to bed at night.

Cut out the pictures and paste them in order on the frames below.
Start with the picture that shows getting up.
Then find the picture that shows what comes next, then next —
all through the day until bedtime.

Pretend that this long strip of paper is a special day
in your life—perhaps your birthday.

Draw pictures to show some of the things you would like to do
on your special day. Begin with the time you get up in the morning
and end with bedtime.

My Name Is _____

13

I CAN!

There are so many things you can do by yourself.
Make an "I CAN" to show how many things you can do.

Color the label on the next page and
draw a picture of yourself in the frame.

Ask an adult to help you find an empty can
that is safe for you to use. Cover the can with the label.

Choose the small pictures that show things you can do.
Cut them out and put them in the can.

Use the empty frames to draw other things you can do.
Be sure to include things you can do to help others.

15

Being Responsible

RESPONSIBLE—What a big word!
It means doing your jobs well.
Use the chart below to show things
that you can do to be responsible.
Check your chart every day to see if
you have done all of your jobs.
Give yourself a star or a smiley face
for each job you have done well.

SOAP! WASH HANDS & FACE								
WATER PLANT								
BRUSH TEETH								
CLEAN PLATE								
FEED PET								
PICK UP TOYS								
DRINK MILK								

Use the empty space at the bottom of the grid to add one more job
of your own choosing.

My Name Is _____

16

HELP!

So many things are going wrong!

What could you do about each problem?
What other people would you call for help?

My Name Is _____

About Families

Families are a very special part of the big world we live in.
They come in many sizes, kinds, and colors.
Can you count the members of each family?

My Name Is _____

Can you tell one very special thing
about each of these families?

My Name Is _____

All Together

This page is reserved for a picture of a very special family . . .
. . . your family!

My Name Is _____

A Family Holiday

Pretend that your whole family will stay together
in this big house for a week.

Cut on the dotted lines to open each door and window.
Now put a little paste around the edges of this page
and paste it on a blank piece of paper the same size.

Fold back the flaps and draw one or more members of the family
in each door and window.

My Name Is _____

Coupon Capers

A coupon is a piece of paper that promises
something special to the person who has it.

THIS COUPON
GOOD FOR

ONE CLEAN PLATE
AT DINNER

by _____

FREE!
one
great big
HUG

compliments of

_ _ _ _ _ _ _ _

GOOD FOR
ONE KISS
from

_ _ _ _ _ _ _ _

free!   this coupon good for   free!

ONE YARD CLEAN-UP

free! by _____ free!

My Name Is _____

As a family member, can you think of
a good way to use each coupon?
Don't forget to write your name on each one.

THIS COUPON
IS GOOD FOR

ONE
CLEAN

BATH TUB

compliments of

_ _ _ _ _ _ _ _ _

promises _YOU_
ONE
FREE
Surprise
☆

this coupon
good for

ONE

QUIET
TIME

SIGNED

_ _ _ _ _ _ _ _

My Name Is _____

Be A Window Watcher!

Select one window in your house
to be your special "Look-Out Place."
Look out the window early in the morning. What color is the sky?
What kind of weather do you think the day will bring?

What do you see in the world outside your window?
Put an X on each box that shows something
you might see in your neighborhood.

In the empty boxes add other things you see in your neighborhood.

My Name Is _____

Pretend these are make-believe glasses.
When you wear them, you can see from your special "Look-Out Place"
things that are really not there!
What would you like to see? Draw it on the lenses of the glasses.

My Name Is _____

Everybody Needs A Home!

Can you help each person or animal
in the picture find the way home?
Trace the lines to connect each creature with its home.

My Name Is _____

27

Oh, Dear!

These children are lost!
Help them find their homes by looking at each one's address.
Draw a line from each child to his or her home.
Then color the picture.

My Name Is _____

This page is for a very special address — your address!
Ask someone to write it lightly for you.
Then trace the letters carefully.

Practice saying your address.

My Name Is _____

Making Friends

Friends are people we enjoy knowing and being close to.
They can be any size, shape, color, age, or nationality.
School is a good place to meet new friends.

Here are some children on their first day of school.

Color the shirt blue of one who looks happy.
Color the clothes yellow of two people who are good friends.

Someone is having trouble. Color his or her shirt red.
Which child do you think will help? Color his or her shirt green.

Which child do you think you would like to have for a friend?

My Name Is _____

Staying Friends

Sometimes things happen that make people feel hurt or angry.
Even good friends can become unhappy with one another.

Look at the picture above and tell what has happened.
Can you think of a way to fix the problem
so that everyone can be happy again?

Finish the cartoon below to show a happy ending.

My Name Is _____

Let's Go!

Trace the streets with your finger to show where each car is going. Tell two things you can do at each place.

At which destination do you think you would spend the most money? Color that car green. Color the car blue in which you would most like to be riding.

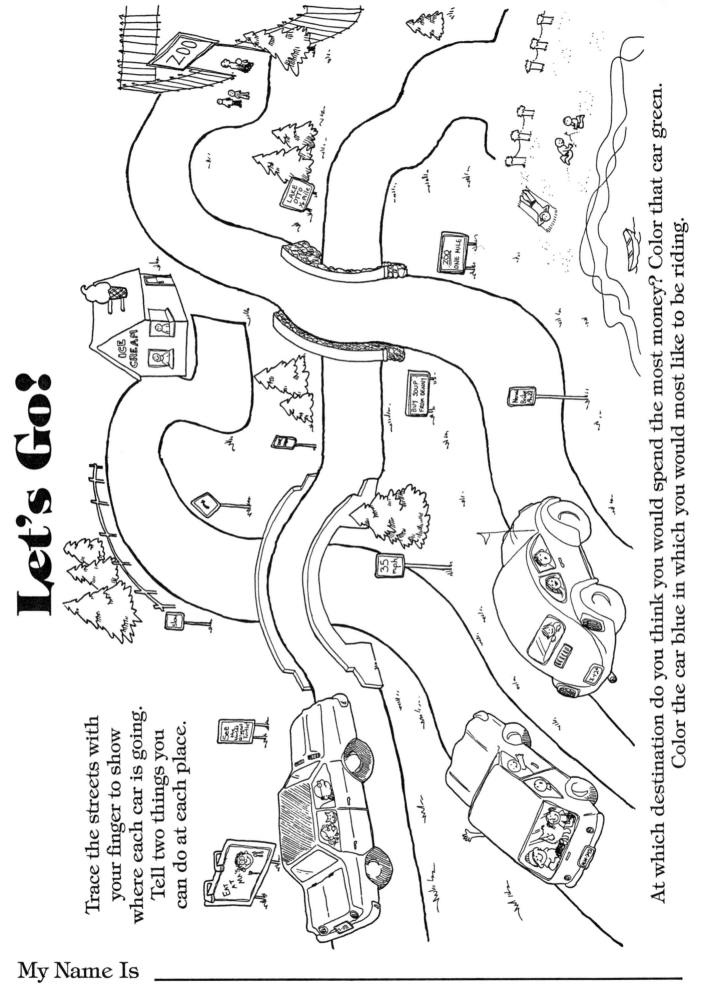

My Name Is _____

Copycat Capers

Use your finger to follow Cornwall the cat on his adventures.
Look at the pictures and tell his story as you go.

My Name Is _____

Let's Go For A Ride!

Cut on the dotted lines.

To match the street lines, paste the two
pages side by side on a big piece of paper.

Color and cut out this car OR
use a toy car of your own.

Pretend to drive your car around this pretend town. Start at home.
Drive your car from home to the steps of the church.

My Name Is _____

Drive from the church to the park.
Can you find two ways to get to the shoe shop?
How many turns must you make to get
from the police station to the ice-cream store?
Plan a trip that will take you from your home
to the school, the pet shop, and the library.

My Name Is _____

Maps Can Tell

There is not enough room on a piece of paper to show how a big piece of the earth really looks. But a map tells us about a place by using **symbols** or simple pictures that look something like the real things.

See if you can tell what these map symbols represent.

1. Color the mountains purple.
2. Color some snow on the highest mountain.
3. Color the hills brown.
4. Color the forest green.
5. Color the river blue.
6. Color the sea blue and green mixed together.

Can you tell what kinds of animals might live in each place on your map?

My Name Is _____

How Do You Go?

How many different ways might you get from your home
to a close friend's house? Circle each way you have traveled.
Put a smiley face by your favorite!

Put an X on the kinds of transportation you could use
to visit a friend who lives in a country across the ocean.

My Name Is _____

Travel Bingo

Make enough copies of the BINGO cards on the next page so that you and your friends can each have one. Everyone will need a crayon.

As you ride or walk, watch for the objects on your BINGO card. When you see one, color in that square.

The winner can be the first to color in a whole row OR the person who has the most colored squares.

Children Of The World

Can you find the places where these children live? Draw a line
connecting each child to a matching symbol that shows where he
or she lives. You will need to use a world map or globe.

Bettina lives
by the sea
in Holland.

Aman lives in a very
hot desert in Egypt.

Pauline lives
on a ranch
in Australia.

Akiko lives in a small
fishing village in Japan.

My Name Is _____

Greg lives near a big, big lake in Canada.

Kara lives in cold, cold Greenland.

Jenny lives on a farm in Iowa, USA.

José lives in a busy city in Mexico.

Marco lives high in the mountains of Peru, South America.

My Name Is _____

Who Lives Here?

Can you tell about the families
who might live in each of these homes?

How is each home like your own home?

How is each one different?

Color the one you would most like to visit.

My Name Is _____

Have You Ever . . .

dreamed about living in a very different kind of house—
perhaps a castle, a cave, or a space capsule?

Draw a picture here of your dream house.
Tell where in the world it would be.

My Name Is _____

43

Every Country Has A Flag

When you salute your country's flag,
you are saying, "I am proud of my country!"

Do you see a picture of your country's flag
on this page? Color your flag.

If your flag is not on this page, use the blank space to draw your flag.

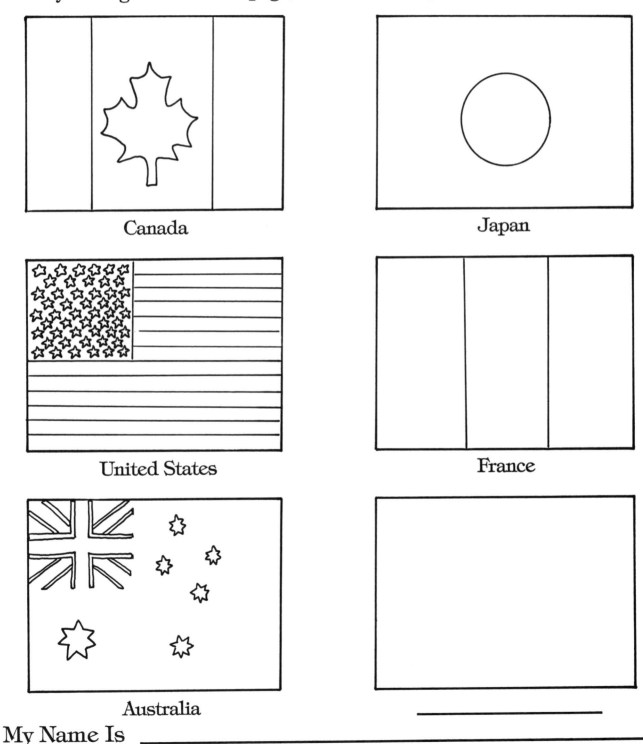

Canada

Japan

United States

France

Australia

My Name Is _____

A Flag For My Country

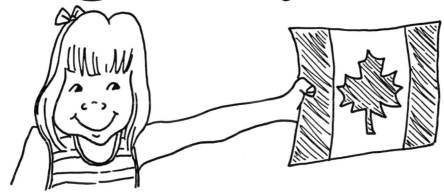

On these pages you will find all of the parts
you will need to make your flag.

To make your flag, you will need:
- a clean piece of paper, about the same size as this page
- scissors, crayons, and paste

Look at the flag parts on these two pages.
Choose **only** the pieces that belong on **your** flag.
Cut, color, and paste the pieces on a blank piece of paper
so that your paper flag looks just like your country's flag.

Peace For All People

October 24 is United Nations Day.
The United Nations is made up of more than 150 countries
which work together for peace for all people of the world.
Almost every country celebrates United Nations Day.

This is the United Nations flag.
The leaves are olive leaves—a very old symbol of peace.
Color the background of the flag **light blue**.
Leave the map and branches **white**.

Cut out the flag and paste it in the center of a clean piece of paper.
Cut on the dotted lines around the people shapes above.
Paste them around the flag.

The Olympic Games

Once every four years, the countries of the world
send their best young athletes to the Olympic games.
The games are held in a different country each time.
The athletes take part in races and contests to see who is the best.
Each winner gets a medal made of gold, silver, or bronze.

Plan your own Olympics.
Get some friends to join you in these races.
Use the pattern below to make some gold medals
for the winners of your Olympic games.

1. Use tagboard or cardboard to make round discs.
2. Cover them with metallic paper.
3. Copy the medallion as many times as needed.
4. Color, cut, and paste a medallion on each disc.
5. Attach a ribbon that will fit over a head.

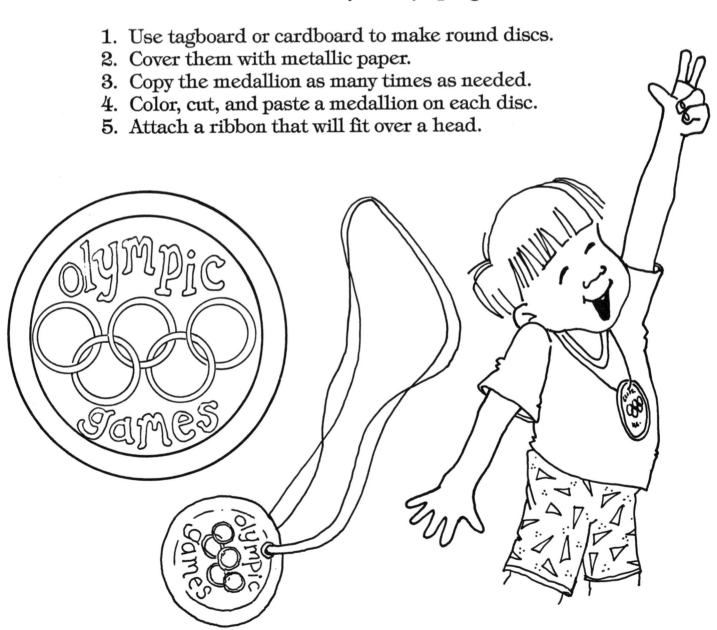

48   © 1995 by Incentive Publications, Inc., Nashville, TN.

Backward Race

This race is run just like an ordinary foot race, except each racer runs BACKWARDS.

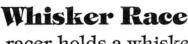

Whisker Race

Each racer holds a whisker (a bent drinking straw) between his or her nose and upper lip. (You may have to curl your lip to hold it tight!) See who can run to the goal and back without losing a whisker.

Hug-A-Ball Relay

This is a partner's race. Place a ball or balloon between your tummy and a partner's tummy. Hug each other tight and move sideways quickly to the goal and back without dropping the ball.

Balloon Blow

Get on your hands and knees. Place a balloon on a starting line. Wet your whistle and blow the balloon gently from the starting line to the finish!

Duck Feather Race

Take off your shoes. Tuck a real or paper feather between two toes of each foot. Walk like a duck from the start to the finish line. Don't lose the feathers or you'll have to begin again!

A Flag Of Friendship

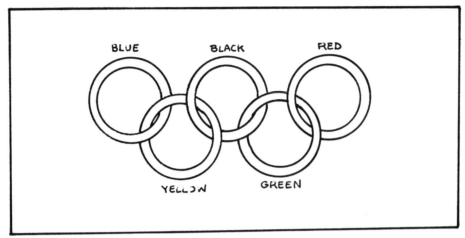

This is the official flag of the Olympic games.

It has five interlocking colored rings on a white background.
The rings represent the five major land areas of the world.
They are interlocked to show friendship between the nations.

At least one of the colors in the Olympic flag
also appears in the flag of every country on earth.
Color the flag.

Now, finish the maze below to see if you can help this flag bearer
carry the flag to its honored place at the Olympic games.

My Name Is _____

Hat Check!

The world is full of interesting people
who have all kinds of different jobs.

Each person in the top row of people
has traded hats with a person in the bottom row.
Draw a line to connect each pair
so that they can reclaim their proper hats.

On a separate piece of paper,
draw yourself wearing a hat that tells
what your favorite job might be.

My Name Is _____

Finders, Keepers!

Fill these scrapbook pages with real things or pictures of things that you would find at home or far away from your home.

Something from my room:

-1-

Something from my neighborhood:

-2-

My Name Is _____

Something
from my town:

Something
from far away:

-4-

Something
from another country:
(where people look and dress differently)

-5-

My Name Is _____

Two Sad Stories

Read the picture stories to see what has happened.

My Name Is _____

In the empty boxes, show at least three things
boys and girls can do to help.

My Name Is _____

It's Up To You

These pictures show boys and girls doing jobs
that will help to keep our world fresh and clean.
Can you tell about each picture?

Which things could you do to help?

My Name Is _____

Pollution Solution

Look at the pictures below.

Make up a story to tell about this kind of pollution.

End your story with a pollution solution.

My Name Is _____

Products On Parade

Each parader belongs in a store.
Can you find the right store for each one?
Draw a line to connect each parader to the right store.

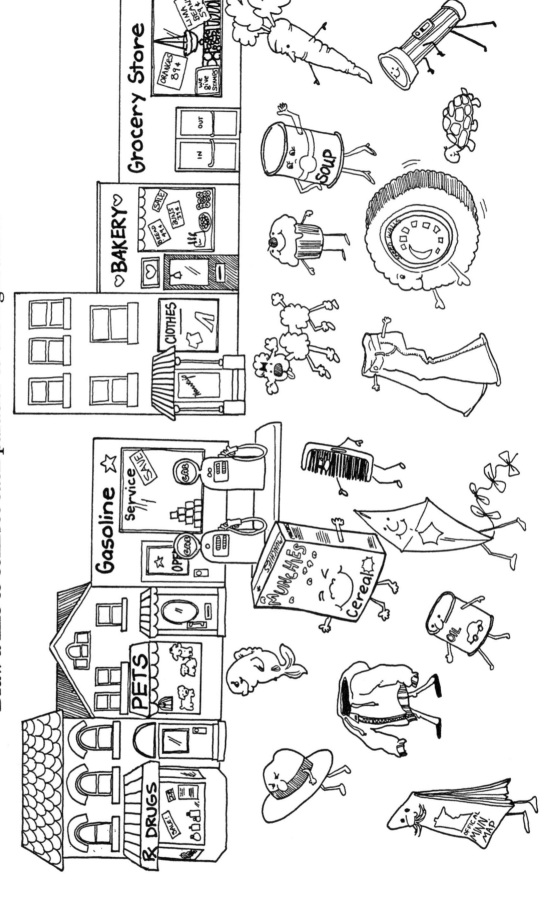

My Name Is _____

58

A World Of Workers

In every city, there are lots of people at work.

How many workers can you name?

If you can name more than ten, you are very alert.

Circle a picture that shows a worker doing something you might like to do someday.

My Name Is _____

Lost Tools

Can you find the lost tools hidden in this picture? Color each tool with a different colored crayon.

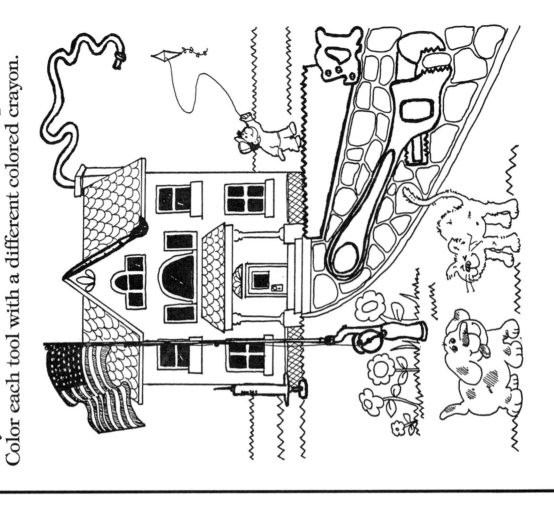

These workers have lost some of their tools.

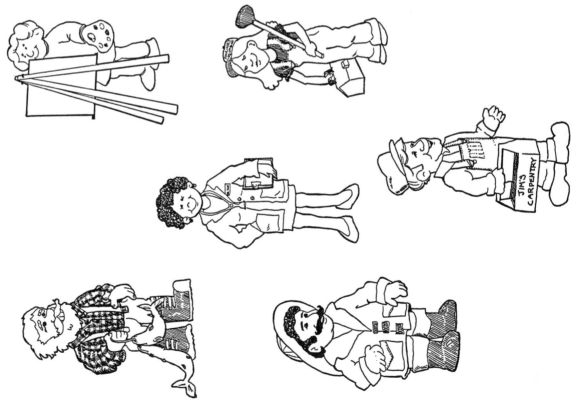

My Name Is _____

Celebrate Inventions

People are the most important part of our world.
The human mind is full of wonderful ideas.
When someone uses an idea to create something brand new,
it is called an **invention**.

On the next page, you will find a list of things that people invented.
Ask your friends to join you in an invention scavenger hunt.
See which group or team can be the first to find all the items.

My Name Is _____

Invention Hunt!

See how many of these inventions you can find.
Collect them in one of the best inventions ever—a paper bag!
Put an X in the box by each item as you find it.

There is one thing on this list that was NOT invented by a person.
Circle its picture.

My Name Is _____

Happy Holidays!

Holidays or festival days are days set aside to celebrate a special event.

It might be a day to honor a national hero or heroine— OR
it might be a time to welcome a new season of the year.
Different countries celebrate different holidays.

Below are pictures or symbols that may remind you of favorite holidays.

See if you can identify each one and tell what holiday it represents.

My Name Is _____

A Holiday To Celebrate Nature

In mid-summer, when the days are long and nights are short, it's fun to stay out late and play. It is the time of year when all the special magic of nature comes alive. Well . . . it isn't really magic, but it's fun to pretend.

In many countries, a mid-summer's eve is when people like to pretend that the woods and hills are filled with good fairies and happy spirits. They pick herbs and flowers to make wreaths. They dance and tell folk tales and fairy stories and celebrate nature.

64

Cut out the flowers on these pages.
Thread a string through the holes
to make a garland for your head or neck.

Tie a silk scarf or some colored tissue
paper streamers to each wrist.
Twist and twirl to show off your streamers.

Take off your shoes and dance like a
woodland fairy.
A song to sing as you dance:
(These words can be sung to *Skip To My Lou*.)
Moon shines brightly, turn and twirl.
Dance so spritely, dip and swirl.
Tiptoe softly; curtsy, then,
Just like the fairies, dance again.

Then make up some stories about your
favorite woodland creatures.

Your Own Special Holiday

Is your name on this list?

John	Jean	Joanna	Johann	Janice
Jan	Joan	Jane	Jon	Joanne
Juan	Jonathan	Juanita	Jana	Joni

If you lived in Spain, you would be a special person on St. John's Day—a holiday that comes in June. On that day, friends would make you special treats such as cakes or cookies in the shape of the letter J.

Plan a Special Names Day holiday for yourself and your friends. Try some of these special events:

1. Use the pattern on the following page to make a crown for the honored person.

2. Use adding machine paper strips to create a shoulder sash that shows your name in big letters. (You might use the colors of your country's flag to decorate the sash.)

3. Get some prepared cookie dough. Flour your hands and roll dough to make a "snake" between your hands. Then shape the snake to make the first letter of your name. Press to flatten and bake 8-10 minutes at 375°. Frost and eat your initial!

4. Sing this song to the tune of *John Jacob Jingleheimer Smith:*

    This is my special holiday
    And I am proud.
    Whenever I go out
    All my friends will shout
    There goes _____! He's (she's) a very special guy (gal)—
                    first name

    dah-dah-dah-dah-dah-dah-dah! (repeat)

My Name Is _____

Write your initial in the medallion on the crown.

Cut out on bold black line. →

Use the strip on the far right side to make crown fit around head.

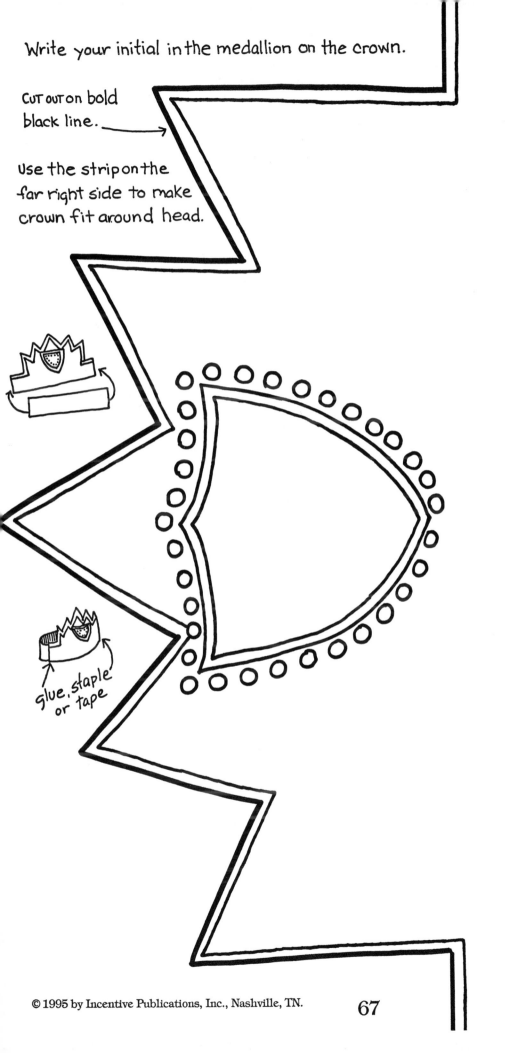

glue, staple or tape

Happy Birthday . . .

These pages are filled with ideas for celebrating a very special day.
Plan a birthday party for yourself!

GLUE

Roll paper into a cone and staple.

Decorate your hat.

MAKE PARTY HATS!

♡ Decorate a paper bag for each person. Tag each bag with a different shape.
Choose 4-6 "treasures" to be hidden for each person. Mark each person's treasures with a different shape tag. Direct the hunters to...

—PLAN A TREASURE HUNT!

My Name Is _____

. . . To You!

MAKE CUPCAKE CONES!

♥ Make your favorite cake batter.
Fill ice-cream cones ⅔ full.
Place on baking sheet.
Bake at 350° for 30-35 minutes.

♥ Cool and frost.

ICE CREAM CONES

FAVORITE CAKE MIX

HAPPY BIRTHDAY!

. . . look only for those treasures tagged with their shape.

DECORATE A BIRTHDAY CHAIR →

My Name Is _____

A Party Puzzle

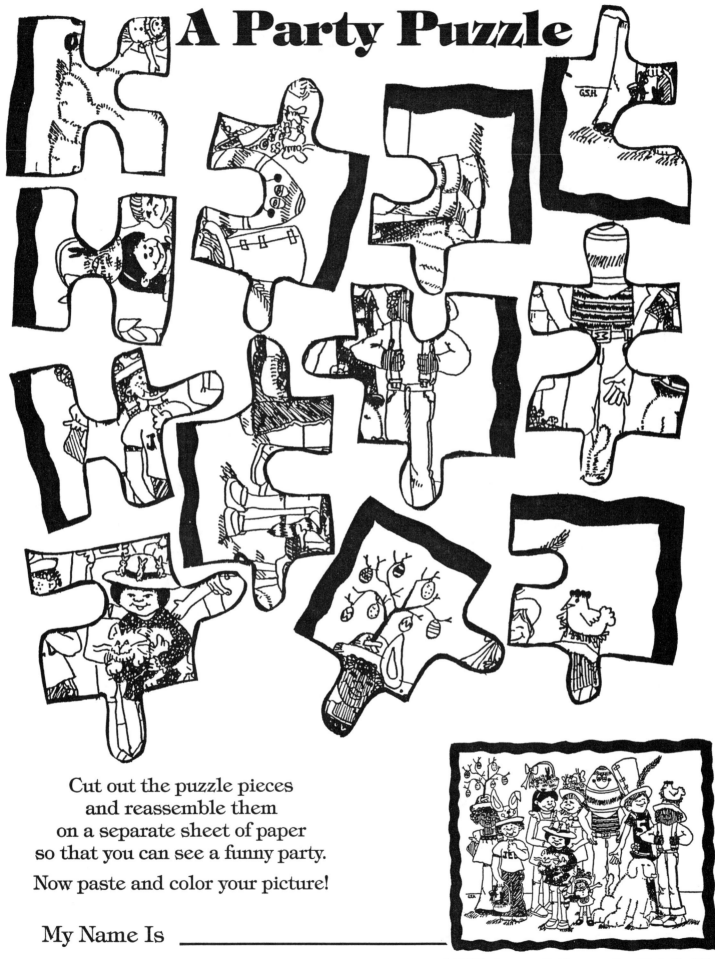

Cut out the puzzle pieces
and reassemble them
on a separate sheet of paper
so that you can see a funny party.

Now paste and color your picture!

My Name Is _____

Old And New

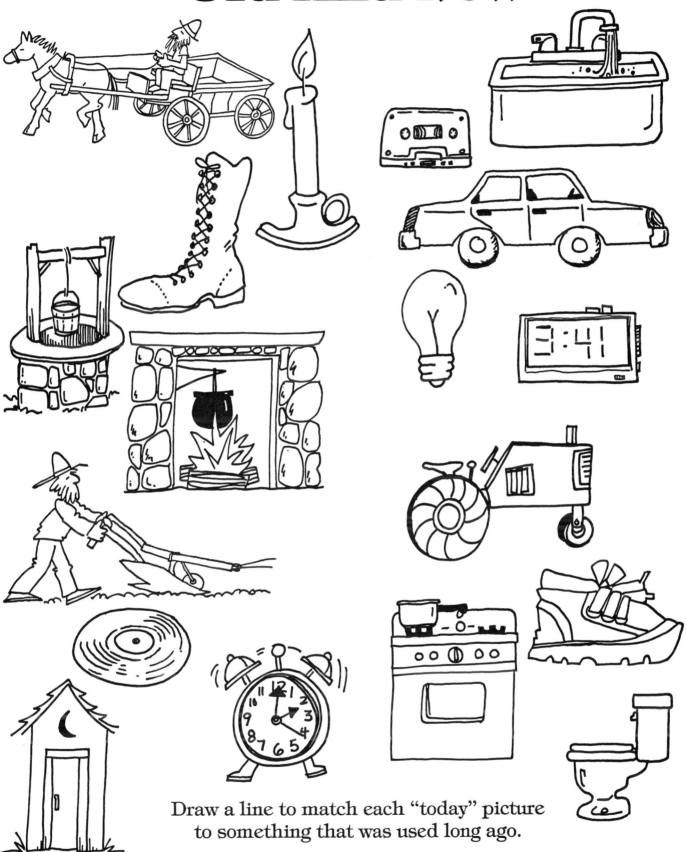

Draw a line to match each "today" picture to something that was used long ago.

My Name Is _____

Time Capsule

Make a time capsule that can be opened on some day in the future. You may want to choose to open it on a special day—perhaps . . . New Year's Day or your birthday or the first day of summer.

Things to put in your time capsule:

- A picture of your family, friends, or pets
- One of your very favorite things
- A page of a magazine or newspaper
- Stuff you carry in your pockets
- Something a friend has given you
- A tape cassette of you talking or singing
- A list of your best friends

Oh, The Things You Can Be . . .

Listen as someone reads
this poem, and imagine
all the things you could
be when you are grown.

When I grow up, I'd like to be
The captain of a ship at sea,
Or pilot jets to far away
And bring them back another day.

Perhaps I'd rather tell the news
And do important interviews,
Write songs or books or poems or plays
Or dance in beautiful ballets.

My Name Is _____

I could be a detective who catches thieves,
Or a gardener who rakes great piles of leaves,
A plumber, a drummer, a daring sky diver,
A mayor, bricklayer, or taxicab driver . . .

An astronaut brave who rockets so high,
Or a master chef who is known for his pie—
A florist, a seamstress, a doctor, a farmer,
A basketball player, or a famous snake charmer.

How will I decide just what I will be?
There are so many jobs. Which one is for me?
Someday I will know, and I'll choose my own.
But today, I'll just **dream**
what I'll be
when I'm grown!

My Name Is _____

74

Learning About Me

Activities To Develop Self-Awareness And Respect For Individual Differences

- Use a space that is easily accessible to children and that will accommodate lively movement in which to set up a learning center to help children become aware of themselves as individuals, each one unique in his or her own way. Provide a large, full-length mirror, if possible, to allow children the opportunity to look at their entire bodies to study distinguishing features and observe growth changes. A chart beside the mirror could include information about each individual, such as height, weight, color of eyes and hair, etc.

- To help children become more conscious of their bodies as ever-changing living and growing things, ask them to bring to class pictures of themselves as babies or toddlers. Take current snapshots of each child and attach them across the bottom half of a bulletin board. Use the top half of the board to display the baby pictures. Leave off any captions, and place the pictures in a random order. Allow time for the children to look at and discuss the two sets of pictures. Have them try to identify the baby pictures by comparing them to the recently taken snapshots. After a reasonable amount of time, rearrange the bulletin board to display the two pictures of each child grouped together with an identifying name tag.

- To further develop the concept of human growth and development, add to the center crayon pictures prepared by each child showing a goal for adult life. Prepare sentence strips to accompany each picture to tell something the child hopes to do. Examples: "Joseph wants to fly airplanes to far-away places." "Susan plans to take ballet lessons and become a famous dancer." "Jenny wants to be a teacher, just like Mrs. Smith." "Sharon will move to the country and grow food to feed hungry people." This activity will be even more fun if the teacher adds his or her own pictures to the board.

- Read the following poem to the children. Then ask them to help you make up actions for the poem as you read it a second time. This action rhyme will become a favorite tension-reliever or warm-up for self-awareness activities as the group memorizes the words and begins to add new lines of their own.

> I'm me, I'm me
> Proud as can be!
> Look the world over
> And you will not see
> A person who fits
> Exactly my size,
>
> Or just the same nose,
> Or just the same eyes.
> From the hair on my head
> To my wiggly toes,
> Everyone knows
> .... I'm me!

- For a lively exercise-oriented activity, have children form a circle to sing and act out the old favorite "Do the Hokey Pokey." Use left hand, right hand, left foot, right foot, and as many other body parts as possible. Urge children to vigorously shake the specified part.

- Declare one day as "Hands On Day." Reinforce the distinction between left and right hands by tying arm bands made of green yarn on the children's left arms and arm bands made of red yarn on their right arms. Then give children corresponding colors of construction paper to trace around their hands to make left and right hands. Help them cut out the hand silhouettes, paste them on a sheet of white construction paper, and label each hand with the appropriate left- or right-hand caption. Completed posters may be displayed around the room to encourage further discussion of left and right.

- Lead a discussion on the importance of learning to use both hands in order to dress and undress one's self without help. Place a big basket of clothing with snaps, buttons, zippers, hooks, and, of course, shoelaces in a spot easily accessible to children. Encourage them to work in pairs to master each of the tasks (zipping, snapping, lacing, and buttoning). Reproduce individual Look awards (page 77) to present to children as they master the independent dressing tasks. This award could be easily modified to reward mastery of other developmentally appropriate tasks, such as counting to a designated number, knowing address and phone number, exhibiting self-control, etc.

LOOK

what I can do!

☐ I can button buttons.

☐ I can lace laces.

☐ I can zip zippers.

☐ I can snap snaps.

Teacher _____

date _____

Learning About The World In Which I Live
Activities To Develop And Reinforce Environmental And Social Awareness

- Choose a window in your classroom from which to look out. Pick out a class tree that can be seen from the window. Watch the tree change from season to season. Several times during the year, take the class outside and walk around the tree. Help children find out the name of the tree. Encourage them to pick up leaves, acorns, nuts, pine cones, or anything else that might have fallen from the tree.

- Plan a field trip around the immediate surroundings to look for litter. Make notes of what you see and where it is located. Due to the risk of contaminated and infectious materials, children should not be allowed to collect the offending debris. Instead, after a discussion of who may have carelessly polluted the area, why they would have done so, and what can be done to prevent future damage, as a group project deliver the notes to the person responsible for maintenance of the area. As a follow-up project, children might make posters promoting personal responsibility for a clean environment.

- Enlist the children's help in mapping the playground. Ask, "What's the shortest way from the slide to the treehouse?" "Find two ways to get from the seesaw to the sandbox."

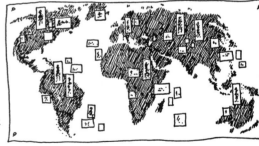

- Secure a large map of the world and attach it to the wall in a conspicuous place. Pin paper dolls dressed in clothing native to their countries on the appropriate spots on the map (coloring books, note cards, calendars, and magazines are good sources of pictures of children around the world). At a later time, ask children to contribute money, postcards, or souvenirs from other countries to be added to the display. Use this display as a springboard for discussion, role playing, or art activities designed to enhance the children's understanding of a wide and wonderful world made up of people with likenesses and differences.

• Make a family album that includes one page for each person in the family. Title the page with that family member's name, add a picture of the person, list something he or she especially likes, and write a sentence about the person (dictated by the child and written by the teacher or a helper). The completed family album would make a special holiday gift for parents or caregivers.

• Help children learn each other's full names and addresses with a manipulative bulletin board designed for independent or teacher-directed free-time use. Address two envelopes for each child in the room. Put one set on the bulletin board, arranged around a construction paper mailbox. Put the second set in a mailbag, and let children match the envelopes.

• Make a chart to be displayed in a prominent place with each child's full name, address, and birth date. Don't forget to celebrate birthdays in a manner appropriate to the group—maybe with a special chair for the birthday child to sit in all day, a special birthday necklace, bracelet, or badge, or birthday cards from the entire group. Whatever method is adopted, it is important to maintain consistency (the same celebration for all birthdays). Don't forget to sing "Happy Birthday" and add a personal wish from the teacher. No day is more special to a child than his or her birthday, and a birthday celebration provides a wonderful opportunity for children to experience the warm glow afforded by sharing another person's happiness.